This Book Belongs To

_____

and I Feel

_____

Let's see how Luke learns how to feel his emotions at the Amusement Park

Luke's semester was coming to a close,
Dad had an idea that he wanted to propose.

"Since summer is close and school's almost done,
Why don't we plan a big outing that will be fun?"
"Maybe," Mom said, "we could go to the beach?"
"Nah," replied Dad, "we did that last week."
They all thought, discussed, and fantasized,
And soon Luke's idea materialized.

"I know what we'll do!" shouted Luke with a joyful cry,
"We could go to Bunny world and try out their rides!
We could play all their games and see Betsy Bunny."
"And if we go on Saturday, it won't cost much money."
After Mom mentioned this, the choice was clear,
Bunny World would be the trip of the year.
Mom and Dad loved it and were soon prepared,
In just a week's time, they all would be there.

Friday at school Luke told his friends,
About his plans for this weekend.
As he and his friends gushed and giggled,
They noticed that Freddy wasn't so tickled.

"You think you're so cool, Luke?" asked Freddy Jackson, "You're giggling over there but I ain't laughin'. If you were really cool then you'd ride the big rides. The Radical Rabbit that has ghosts inside."

"G-ghosts?" cried Luke, "That can't be real!"
"Oh," said Peter "it's the real deal!
If you wanna be cool, then ride it and see,
Or else I'll call you a big ol' baby."

These words bothered Luke, but he had to stay strong,
"I'll ride that ride, Freddy, all day long!
So don't even think that I'm scared of ghosts,
Once that ride is through, that thing'll be toast!"

As Freddy stomped away angry and steaming,
Luke and friends were giggling and beaming.
He wanted Freddy to be jealous and eat his words,
Luke thought that he could easily steel his nerves.
But Luke didn't know the challenges that lay ahead,
And he would regret all the things that he'd said.

The day of the park had finally arrived,
Luke struggled to keep his excitement inside.
He did all his chores and homework too,
Then he dressed and put on his new white shoes.

Once Luke knew Mom and Dad were ready,
He jumped in the car, holding his teddy.
Luke thought of all the fun they'd have today,
He thought of the ice cream and games they'd play.

But then his worst fear was mentioned by Mom,
"I'd like to see the fireworks!" But Luke tried to stay calm.
Fireworks made Luke shiver and shake,
He felt like he'd been in a major earthquake.

"M-Mom?" squeaked Luke in a nervous voice,
"I don't like those." He said as his head became moist.
"Oh!" said Mom, "You're still scared of those, dear?"
"Yes," replied Luke, "they're my biggest fear!"

"But, dear," said Mom, "please give them a try,
They're the best thing I've ever seen with my own eyes."
But Luke was insistent so they refrained,
"Well, that's alright, honey. We'll just play lots of games!"

The amusement park was lit by the setting sun,
The 'Bunny World' sign felt inviting and fun.
Mom, Dad, and Luke were having a blast.
They felt so relaxed, having fun at last.

Mom and Luke tried some rides,
Laughing as they rode, until it split their sides.
Dad won every single game that he tried,
Winning the biggest and best prizes inside.

As the family walked further into the park,
Luke's happy eyes soon became dark.
He saw the ride that he'd been dreading,
Towards the Radical Rabit was where he was heading.

RADICAL RABIT

The line was long and the ride looked scary,
So Luke started sweating and felt very weary.
But he wobbled ahead toward certain doom,
Filled to the brim with fear and gloom.

"Woah there, son," said Dad quickly,
"Where are you goin'? You're not old enough, silly!"
"But Dad," he cried "I have to go!
This is more important than you even know."
He confessed the challenge and his attempt to impress,
Luke wanted so badly to be considered the best.

"Son," said Dad, "Don't try making your friends jealous,
It won't make you happy if you're acting reckless.
If you're doing something too scary, it's better to stop.
Now, why don't we go and ride that one — the Bunny Hop?"

Luke saw the ride and thought it seemed fun,
He rode it with his mom and loved how it spun!

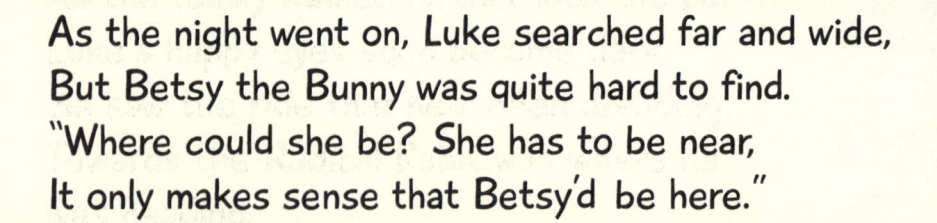

As the night went on, Luke searched far and wide,
But Betsy the Bunny was quite hard to find.
"Where could she be? She has to be near,
It only makes sense that Betsy'd be here."

The amusement park lights weren't very bright,
But Luke still caught a figure in his sights.
It was Betsy the Bunny, but she wasn't small,
Oh no, it seemed Betsy was much too tall.

The dim light made Betsy look frightening,
Luke was shocked and felt his chest tightening.
"Mom!" cried Luke, "It's Betsy Bunny!
But she doesn't seem nice or very funny."
He stood behind mom to safely hide,
So Mom took him to a corner to talk aside.

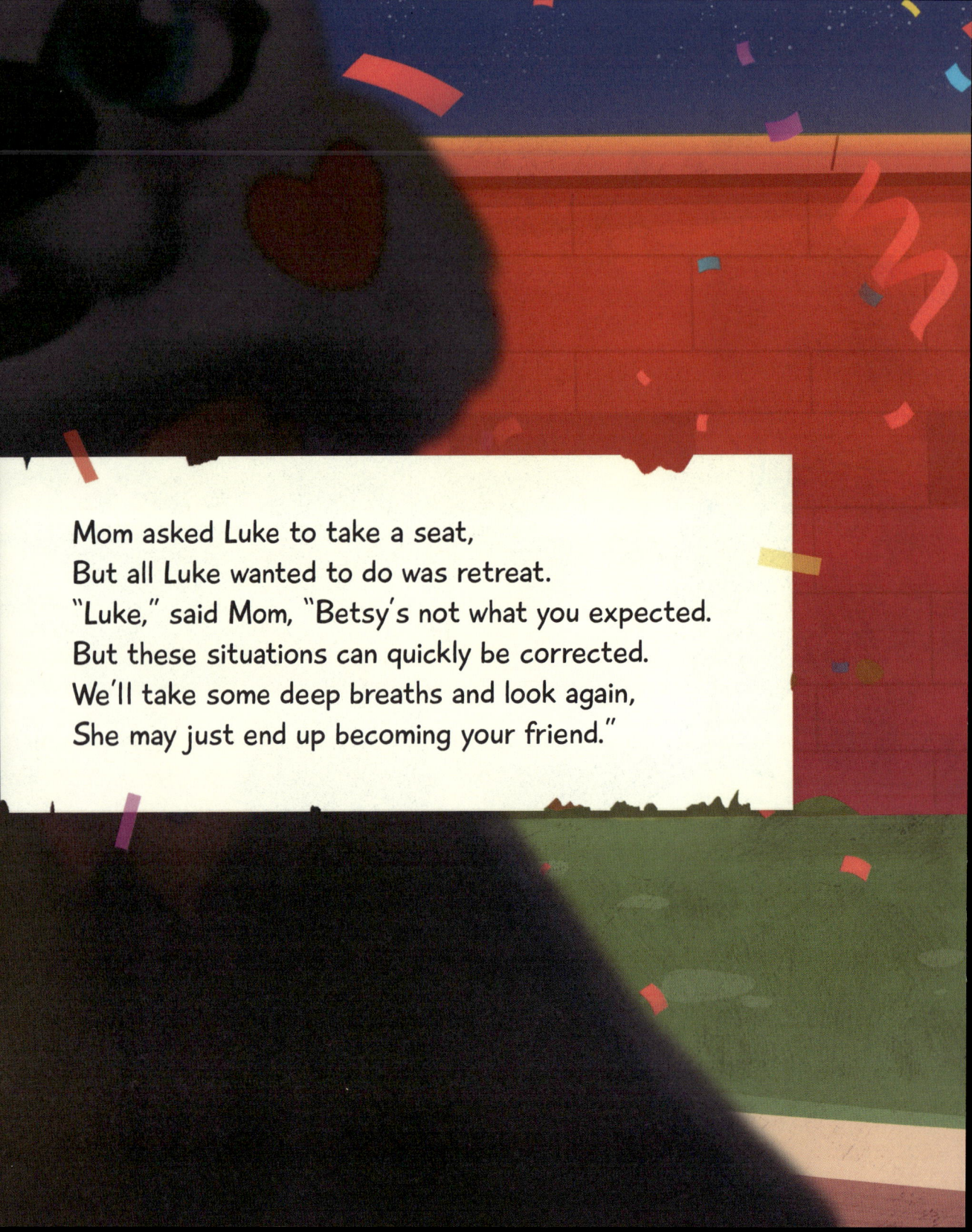

Mom asked Luke to take a seat,
But all Luke wanted to do was retreat.
"Luke," said Mom, "Betsy's not what you expected.
But these situations can quickly be corrected.
We'll take some deep breaths and look again,
She may just end up becoming your friend."

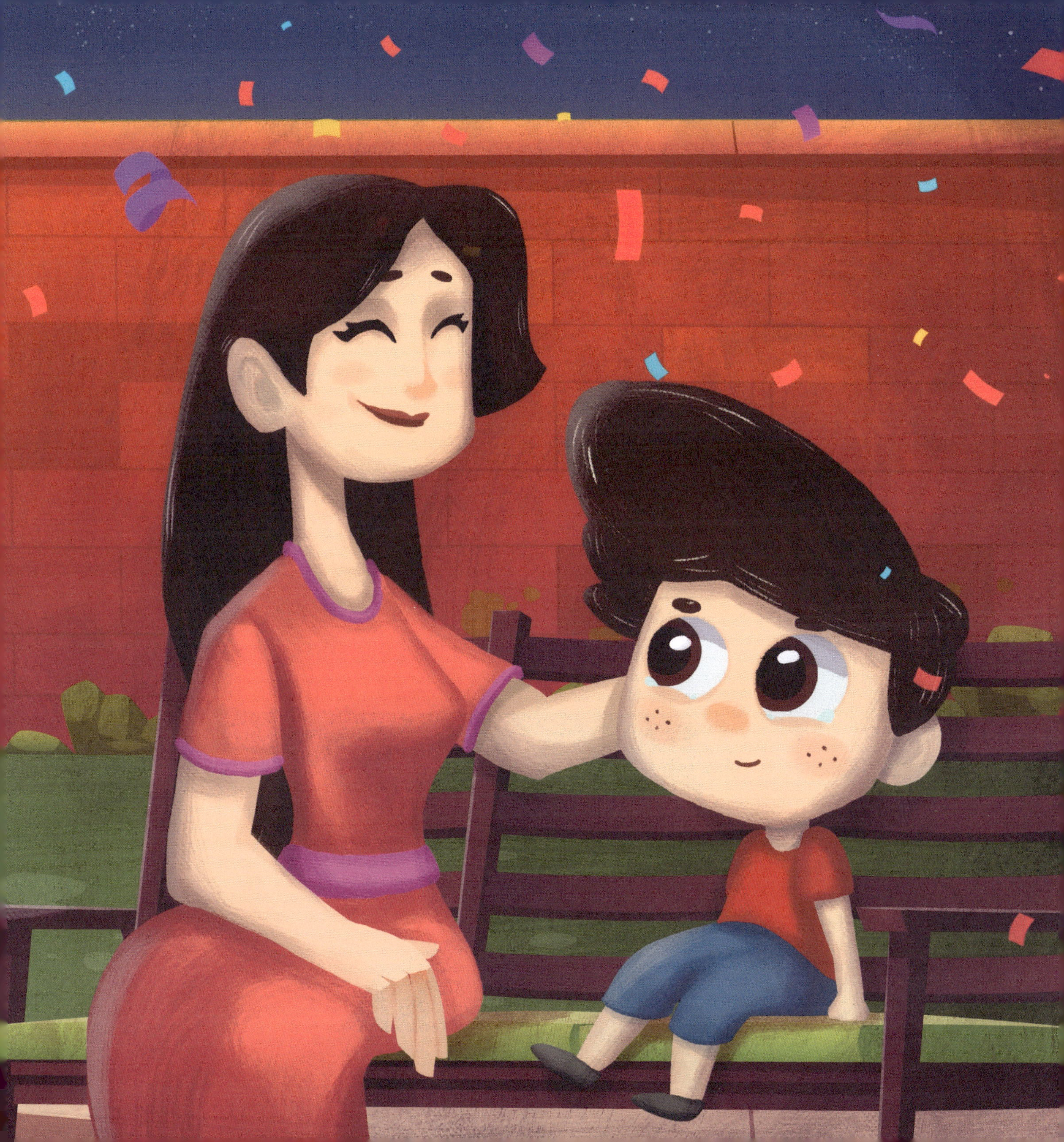

Luke looked again in Betsy's direction,
She seemed much nicer upon further inspection.
Her fur was fluffy, bright, and kinda pinky,
Her eyes were blue and sorta twinkly.

Some of Luke's fear had left his mind,
So he decided to try to be kind.
"H-Hello, Betsy," said Luke with a stutter,
She waved hello with a finger flutter.

It made Luke laugh and feel a little better,
So the family and Betsy took a picture together.
After a while, Luke forgot his concerns,
And all of the excitement he felt soon returned.

We have to head out before the fireworks show."
Luke thought for a moment about all he achieved,
He thought it'd be sad to just simply leave.
He'd become so brave all in one day,
"Actually," said Luke, "do you think we could stay?"

"Luke!" said Dad, "Have you overcome your fear?
Is that the reason you want to stay here?"
"I've done so much and grown some too,
And I'd like to see the fireworks with you."

So the family got ice cream and drove up a hill,
Where they could see the whole park and fireworks still.
Luke was a little nervous but had summoned courage,
So he wouldn't let his feelings keep him discouraged.

A single firework flew into the sky,
He'd never seen colors like those up high.
Though the sound was loud, he didn't care,
As the fireworks show glittered everywhere.

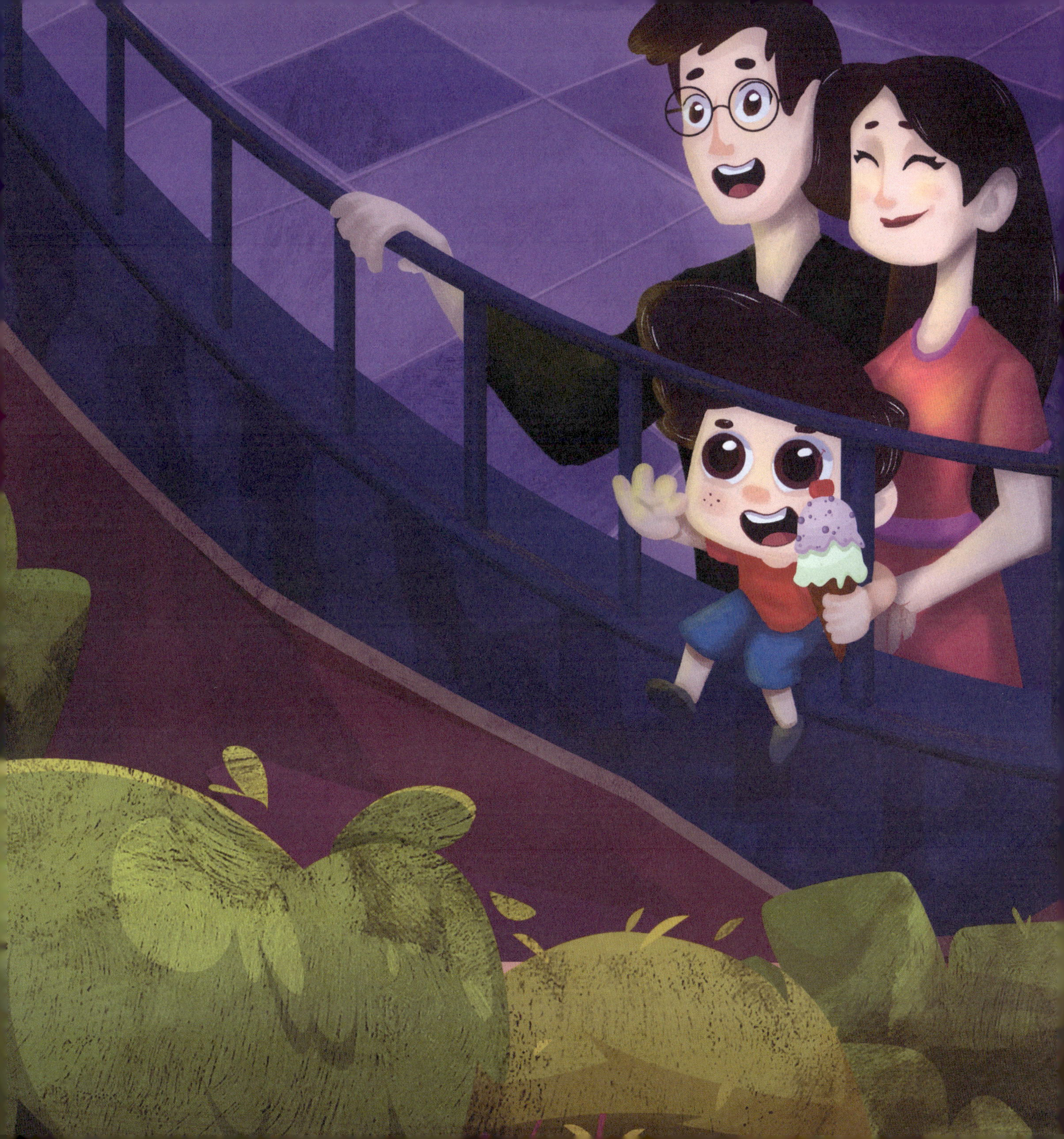

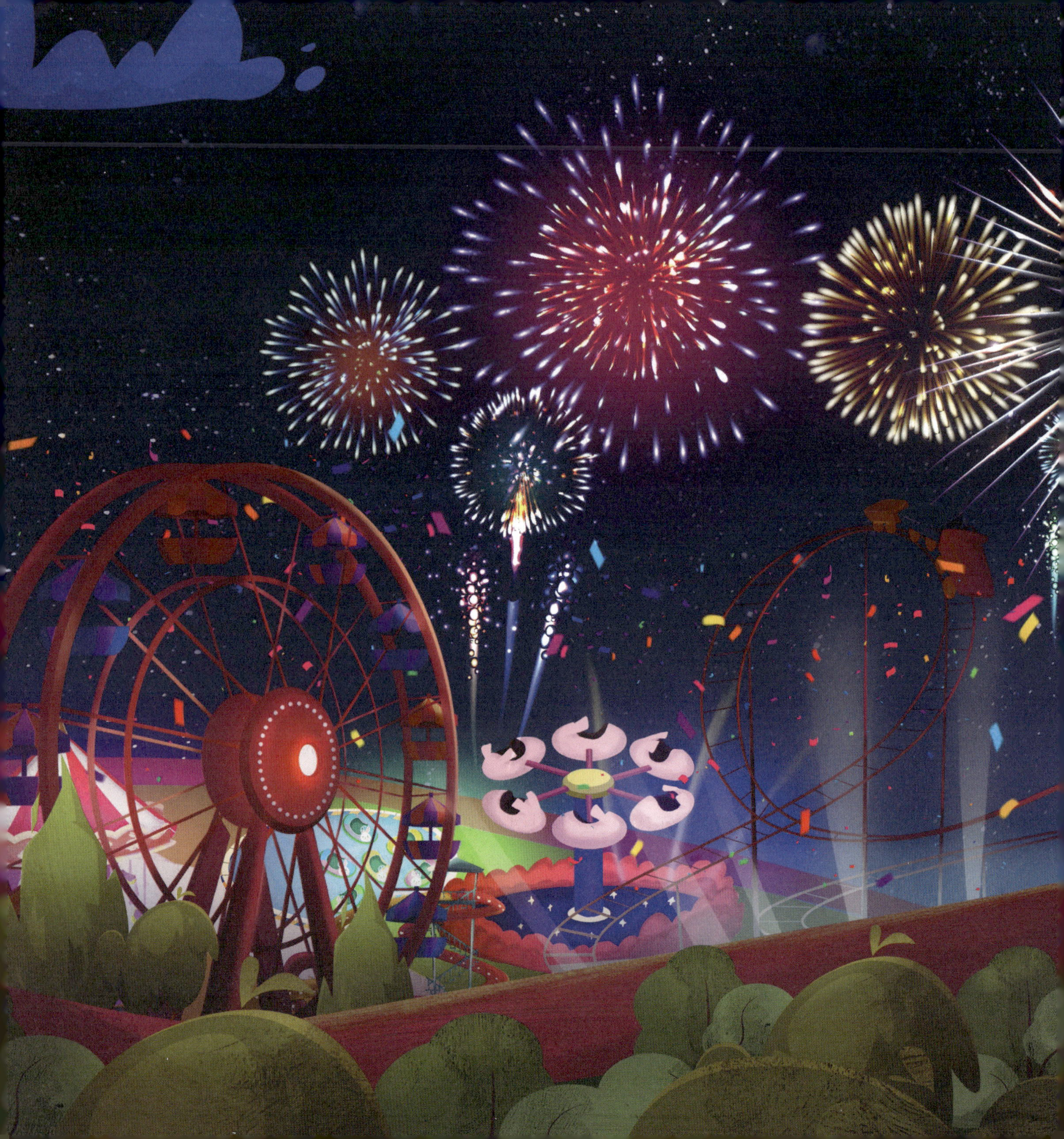

Then he looked on the display below, "This is so great! I didn't know!"

As they all drove home from their big day,
Mom was proud and Dad had lots to say,
"We're proud of you for being so brave,
You made some good choices and were well behaved.
It's good to stay calm in every situation,
Whether you're at school or on vacation.
Thinking things through or even saying no,
Are both great paths and ways to go."

"Are you okay?" asked Mom, "You haven't made a peep."
But when she turned around he'd fallen fast asleep.

THE END

Do you want a surprise?
We have a free gift that will make you enjoy
this book even more.

Send an email at hello@mariellasanders.com
with the name of the book, and we'll arrange the rest.

More books in the collection:

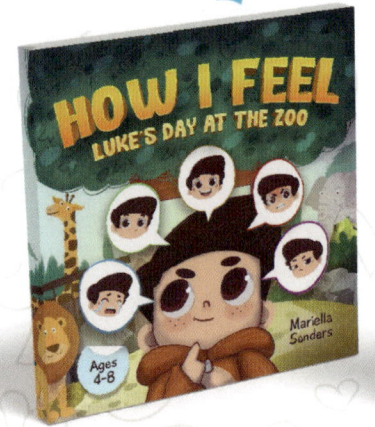

Luke's Day at
The Zoo

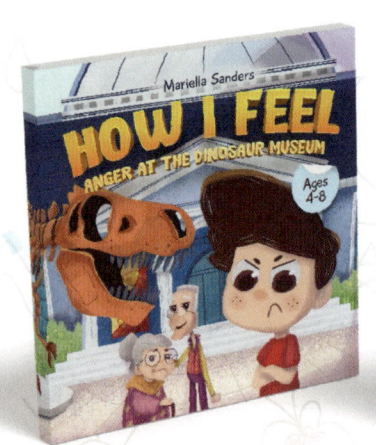

Anger at The
Dinosaur Museum

and many
more to go...

Discover our New Books at

www.mariellasanders.com

Printed in Great Britain
by Amazon